Written by David F. Marx

Illustrated by Jeff Shelly

Children's Press®
A Division of Grolier Publishing
New York • London • Hong Kong • Sydney
Danbury, Connecticut

To my wife, Christine
— J. S.

Reading Consultant
Katharine A. Kane
Education Consultant
(Retired, San Diego County Office of Education
and San Diego State University)

Visit Children's Press® on the Internet at:
http://publishing.grolier.com

Library of Congress Cataloging-in-Publication Data
Marx, David F.
    Turn it off! / by David F. Marx ; illustrated by Jeff Shelly.
      p. cm. – (Rookie reader)
    Summary: A child slowly realizes all that is being missed by watching too
much television.
    ISBN 0-516-22229-5 (lib. bdg.)   0-516-27296-9 (pbk.)
    [1. Television—Fiction.] I. Shelly, Jeff, ill. II. Title. III. Series.
PZ7.M36822 Tu 2001
[E]—dc21   00-030696

© 2001 by Children's Press®, a Division of Grolier Publishing Co., Inc.
Illustrations © 2001 by Jeff Shelly
All rights reserved. Published simultaneously in Canada.
Printed in the United States of America.
1 2 3 4 5 6 7 8 9 10 R 10 09 08 07 06 05 04 03 02 01

Do you watch too much TV?

Turn it off!

Are you up too late?

Does your body ache?

8

9

Is your homework done?

11

Is your brother having fun?

Is that movie too scary?

Are your eyes tired of staring?

18

Are your friends outside?

Will you miss your ride?

21

Turn it off!
Turn it off!

Turn it off!

Turn it off!

If you turn it off . . .

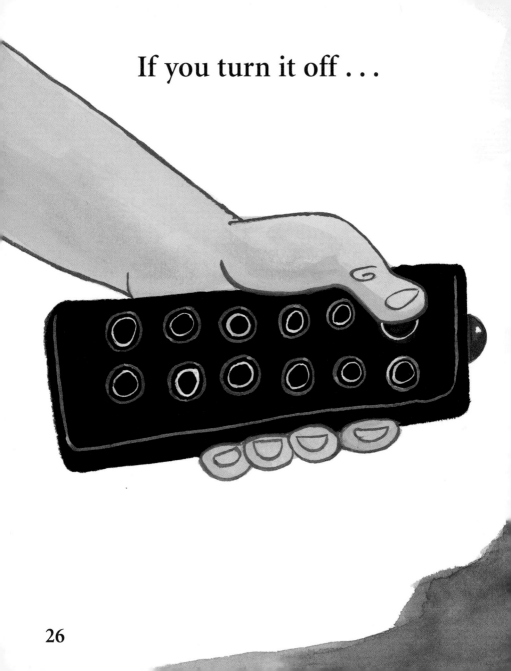

and LEAVE it off . . .

you will always find
something going on.

31

Word List (42 words)

ache	having	ride
always	homework	scary
and	if	something
are	is	staring
body	it	TV
brother	late	that
do	leave	tired
does	miss	too
done	movie	turn
eyes	much	up
find	of	watch
friends	off	will
fun	on	you
going	outside	your

About the Author

David F. Marx is a children's author and editor who lives in suburban Chicago. He is the author of several other books in the Rookie Reader and Rookie Read-About Geography series for Children's Press.

About the Illustrator

Jeff Shelly is a humorous illustrator. Born in Lancaster, Pennsylvania, he currently resides with his wife, Christine, and two dachshunds, Jessie and James, in Hollywood, California.